Solitaire & Double Solitaire

Solitaire & Double Solitaire

BY ROBERT ANDERSON

 Random House · New York

Anderson, Robert Woodruff, 1917–
Solitaire & Double solitaire.

Two plays.
I. Anderson, Robert Woodruff, 1917–   Double solitaire. 1972. II. Title. III. Title: Double solitaire.
   PS3501.N34S6 1972   812'.5'4   78-37029

. . . to the Memory of John Gassner

SOLITAIRE/DOUBLE SOLITAIRE *was first presented in New Haven at the Long Wharf Theater by the Long Wharf Theater Company. It opened February 12, 1971. The Company subsequently traveled to Edinburgh for the 1971 Edinburgh International Festival.* SOLITAIRE/DOUBLE SOLITAIRE *opened in Edinburgh September 6, 1971. The Company opened on Broadway at the John Golden Theater on September 30, 1971.*

DIRECTOR	Arvin Brown
SETS	Kert Lundell
COSTUMES	Lewis Rampino
LIGHTING	Ronald Wallace

Cast for SOLITAIRE

SAM BRADLEY	Richard Venture
MADAM	Ruth Nelson
DAUGHTER	Patricia Pearcy
BROTHER	Will Fenno
WIFE	Joyce Ebert
FATHER	John Cromwell
CAPTAIN	William Swetland

Cast for DOUBLE SOLITAIRE

CHARLEY	Richard Venture
BARBARA	Joyce Ebert
MRS. POTTER	Ruth Nelson
MR. POTTER	John Cromwell
SYLVIA	Martha Schlamme
GEORGE	William Swetland
PETER	Will Fenno

Solitaire & Double Solitaire

We are aware of a dimly lighted cell-like room measuring about eight feet square. A man of about fifty comes from the shadows and approaches the entrance to the cell. The door panel slides open, and he enters.

Immediately bright lights snap on. Along one side of the Servocell is a slab which serves as a bed. On another wall are a number of computer buttons and knobs and what looks like a television screen. The man is dressed in some oufit of the future. He carries a small knapsack with all his personal belongings.

RECORDED MALE VOICE Register, please! . . . Register, please! . . . Register, please!

SAM (*Obediently*) Samuel Thomas Bradley. 1783.965.281 Stroke 6A . . . IQSQC 240. No address. Employed by Central Library to record books on tape.

RECORDED MALE VOICE Your voice signature does not correspond to the signature on record at Central.

SAM I have a slight cold.

MALE VOICE Verify by means of Lifetime Identification Card. (SAM *obediently slips the card into the slot*) Welcome to International Servocell. (SAM *proceeds to take off his jacket and fold it neatly, take out his possessions and place them neatly on a shelf, and remove his boots*) May we remind you at this time that no person may occupy the same Servocell for more than twenty-four hours. When your time is up, an alarm will sound, giving

3

you five minutes to leave before the automatic cleaning system goes into operation, sterilizing the Servocell for the next occupant.

RECORDED FEMALE VOICE   Please adjust the volume so that you will not disturb the occupants of the Servocells on either side of you or below or above you.

MALE VOICE   The Servocell is now at your Service.
(SAM *now takes a small slide from his knapsack and places it in a slot in the computer wall. A picture of a pretty woman holding a dog comes up on screen.* SAM *stands and looks at it for a moment*)

FEMALE VOICE   You will notice that the services are indicated by representative symbols and by legends for those older people who still read. So that we may program the Services for your pleasure and convenience, please indicate on the panel your age, and whether you are man, woman, heterosexual or homosexual.
(SAM *obediently pushes the appropriate buttons, and starts trying to adjust the temperature by turning a knob on the panel*)

MALE VOICE   You may control the temperature in your room for your maximum comfort by manipulating the temperature control dials on the master panel.
(SAM *has held his handkerchief up to the vents. It hangs limp*)

SAM   They don't work. There's not a breath of air in this room. And the television doesn't work. It didn't work in the cell I had last night either.

FEMALE VOICE   May we remind you at this time of the opportunity offered for early self-disposal before the

4

mandatory age of sixty. (SAM *pushes a button, and a washbasin swings out from the panel, or rises in the corner*) If you should decide on early self-disposal, push the lavender button for instructions. (SAM *washes his hands*) Those with combined Intelligence Quotient-Sperm Qualification Counts of between 250 and 300 are required to leave their weekly quota of sperm before the early self-disposal system will operate. Those with IQSQC of over 300 are not allowed to avail themselves of early self-disposal.

(*Pause*)

MALE VOICE You have an unpaid bill of sixty-nine dollars and fifty-two cents at the store.

SAM No. No. I do not. I've sent you numerous tapes on this subject.

ANOTHER MALE VOICE Please do not raise your voice. It confuses the delicate mechanism of the Servocell Electronic Brain Center.

SAM (*Whispering*) Doesn't the computer pay any attention to any of the tapes we send in over there?
> (*He has finished washing. The basin retracts. He is now ready for the evening's procedure. He selects his "liquor card" from his belongings and inserts it in a slot in the panel*)

MALE VOICE You have used up your quota of intoxicants for this week.
> (SAM *stands there for a moment, absorbing this sad news*)

ANOTHER MALE VOICE You may have an unlimited supply of drugs and intoxicants if you elect early self-

5

disposal. If you decide to select this plan, push the lavender button for further information.

(SAM *is about to lie down on the slab, but is caught mid-way by the next voice*)

MALE VOICE   Our records indicate that you have not deposited your quota of sperm for this week, as required by all men with a rating of over 200.

SAM (*Anguished*)   I can't do that any more. I am no animal . . . Please, I want to speak to somebody in charge.

MALE VOICE   Please do not raise your voice. It confuses the delicate mechanism of the Servocell Electronic Brain Center.

(SAM *sits depressed for a long time . . . He looks over the various buttons on the panel. No hope, no amusements there . . . He finally pushes a button*)

FEMALE VOICE   This is a recording. All the doctors at Central Counselling are occupied. You may either signal back later or record your problem at the sound of the bleep, and the counsellors will handle your case as soon as possible. (*A moment's pause . . . and then a bleep. Sam is tongue-tied by the necessity of speaking on signal, and the heaviness of his heart. He doesn't really make any effort to speak . . . After a few moments, another bleep*) The doctors will consider your problem as soon as possible. Meanwhile we are activating the Marriage-Minus-One tapes in your cell. May we remind you that these tapes are available for purchase at the store. Our selections for today are "Husband Comes Home," "Christmas Eve," "Bedtime" and "Cocktail Party."

WIFELY VOICE   Is that you, Honey? (SAM *has heard this a hundred times and just lies there*) Did you have a good day? (*He snorts at the idea*) Dinner's almost ready. It was a lovely day, wasn't it? (*There is, of course, a pause between the questions for the other half of the conversation. But Sam does not respond*) The man came to fix the television set but he said it couldn't be fixed. We'll have to get a new one. You'd better get yourself a drink or smoke a little grass before I tell you some of the other things that happened. (SAM *suddenly thinks that since everything is fouled up in the cell, the liquor slot might work this time. He sits up and gets his liquor card*) Oh, anything at all. Get your feet up and enjoy your drink. I'll be in in a few minutes.

(SAM *inserts the liquor card*)

MALE VOICE   You have used up your quota of intoxicants for this week.

SAM   Nothing else in this damned place works but this.

WIFELY VOICE   I'll be in for my drink in a minute, dear. (*He shuts her off and is just lying down to nap again*)

MALE VOICE   Register, please! . . . Register, please! (SAM *just looks at the panel, shakes his head*) Register, please.

SAM (*Resigned*)   Samuel Thomas Bradley. 1783.965.281 Stroke 6A . . . IQSQC 240. No address. Employed by Central Library to record books on tape. And I have a slight cold because the Servocell I slept in last night was freezing.

MALE VOICE   Your voice signature does not correspond to the signature on record at . . . (SAM *is ready for this, and shoves the identification card in the slot, thereby choking off the rest of the speech*) *Welcome to International Servocell.*

(SAM *turns down the volume, and lies on the cot*)

7

FEMALE VOICE This is a recording from Central Counselling. The problem you consulted us about falls into a broad category of complaints, and in the interest of efficiency is being answered by this tape.

MALE VOICE The Counsellors recommend that you purchase Dr. Richard Morrison's latest tape, "New Ways in Autoeroticism." . . . Be well!

SAM Thanks a lot, you stupid bastard. That's your answer to everything. New ways to turn on, new ways to—

FEMALE VOICE (*Interrupting*) Dinner is now being served. (*Sam is not really hungry*) Dinner is now being served. . . . Dinner is now being served.
      (*To quiet her and out of desperation,* SAM *pushes the lighted button*)

ANOTHER FEMALE VOICE Chicken patty . . . Veal patty . . . (*Bleep*) . . . Fish patty.

SAM What happened to the beef patty? (*Pushes button again*)

FEMALE VOICE Chicken patty . . . Veal patty . . . (*Bleep*) . . . Fish patty. Your records indicate high cholesterol. Beef has been removed from your diet until further notice.
      (*With very little interest,* SAM *pushes a button. An Automat-like door opens and we see a glob of something, a cup and a fork, all wrapped in cellophane. He looks at the sterile mess and takes them to his cot and puts them down. He then goes to the panel and turns a knob, which lowers the lights. He gets a tape from his possessions, and talks to the picture of his wife showing on the panel*)

SAM Hello, Honey. Oh, God, how I miss you. It's terrible. You said it would be. I know they wouldn't have let us stay together. Nobody's together any more. But just to have known you were alive someplace . . . that perhaps I might be in the same cell you were in the night before. For all their sterilizing I do occasionally find a hairpin. . . . The Union man caught me working today. I wasn't supposed to be working. I'd worked my one day this week. Now I won't be allowed to work for three months . . . I keep getting money, of course. That's guaranteed. But not to be allowed to work even that one . . . miserable . . . day . . . I've about worn out our tapes. But they help.

(*He slips a tape into another slot in the panel*)

FLORENCE (*On tape*) Hello, darling. Are you home?

SAM (*On tape*) Yes, I'm here.

FLORENCE Did you shop for dinner?

SAM Yes. I knew you'd be late . . . How are you?

FLORENCE (*Kissing and snuggling*) Mmmm. I hate it when they keep me late at the office. Get out of the kitchen. I don't want you in here.

SAM I don't mind. I like to cook.

FLORENCE But I mind. I'm getting fat on your cooking. Nothing but cream sauces.

SAM You taught me how to make it.

FLORENCE Well, I wish I hadn't. Now come on, get out. I'm going to make dinner.

SAM (*Seductive*) Why don't we let dinner wait?

FLORENCE   Aren't you hungry?

SAM   Yes.
(*He makes it clear it's a different kind of hunger*)

FLORENCE (*Laughing*)   Oh, you're impossible.

SAM   You love it, and you know it.
(SAM *has been sitting listening to the tape, remembering. It has made him more miserable instead of comforting him as it sometimes does. In the middle of Florence's last words, he jumps up and yanks out the tape.*
After a long moment, he looks at his untouched food, pushes another button, and a disposal unit opens. He drops the mess down the unit and it closes.
Nothing works tonight for him. He leans against the panel for a while . . . then looks over at the lavender self-disposal button, which has been glowing since he entered the cell. Finally he pushes it)

MAN'S VOICE   In choosing early self-disposal, you have made the most important decision of your life.

SAM   Don't worry, Florence, I'm not going to do it. But sometimes it helps me to get through a bad night, to think I might do it. That I could do it if I wanted to.

FEMALE VOICE   Please listen carefully to conditions and instructions. There are a series of steps indicated by the buttons. You may change your mind at any of the steps except the last . . . The first step. Place any valuables you may wish to leave for the Archives at Central, with recorded instructions . . . Step Two. A brief opportunity to record your feelings for posterity. Step Three, and from here on your choice is irrevocable. You will be given a pill and a glass of water. Then lie on the cot, and that is all. Please carry anything you do not leave for the Archives onto the cot with you, as you must leave the Servocell in a neat and tidy condition for the next occupant.

SAM (*Smiles at this*) I sometimes wonder how you ever made it, Florence . . . How you ever managed to get all that junk you used to carry around with you on the cot.

(*Sam presses the first button*)

FEMALE VOICE Review the valuables you may have with you. Those you want to pass on to the Archives, place in a compartment which will now open.

(*A small lighted vault opens.* SAM *looks at it but makes no move to do anything. He presses the next button*)

FEMALE VOICE Last words if you wish. At the sound of the beep, you may talk for approximately three minutes . . .

(SAM *pushes the next button*)

FEMALE VOICE This is a warning. When you push the next button, the rest is irrevocable and automatic.

SAM (*Long pause*) This moment always excites me, Florence . . . It's the only moment of the day when I really feel alive. (*He plays around the button with the tip of his finger, as one might cock a pistol and point it at one's head. Finally he shakes his head sadly—goes to his coat and gets out his phone*) Hello, my name is Samuel Thomas Bradley. My charge plate number with you is 668–4 . . . I've used your service in other cities and I wonder . . . I know it's very short notice, but I wonder if you could take care of me tonight . . . But I'm desperate . . . Well, I'm more desperate than most people . . .

I think . . . Just for a short while . . . Till ten? . . .
That would be fine . . . Well, I don't think I'll ask too
much of you. I'm fifty-two, and I would like her to be
around twenty-four, twenty-five . . . Well, any age you
have, then . . . Light hair. Medium size . . . Two children, if you can make it. Teen-agers. Boy and girl if
possible . . . Fried chicken and green salad . . . I'd like
the kitchen if you could arrange it . . . And if they
could play a little cards. That's not necessary, but if it's
possible.

> (*The Servocell set has moved off as* SAM *has stepped
> from it . . . And at the end of the speech,* THE
> MADAM *enters in limbo*)

THE MADAM Did you say you wanted a dog?

SAM If possible.

THE MADAM We have two dogs, but I'm afraid they're
being used by other families tonight. I started this
operation, you know, back before The System, as a
Call Dog Service. I found that many people wanted a
dog just for the weekend. Didn't want to bother with
it all the time, so I started a kennel and rented Call
Dogs. Then when The System took over, and marriage and family went by the boards, I found people
sometimes had a craving for a family for an evening or
a special event. So I started Call Families.

SAM Well, it's saved my life on many occasions.

THE MADAM Of course it's getting harder to train the
Staff, to teach them what a family was like. We've just
about worn out our Andy Hardy movies . . . Now you
understand . . . no sex.

SAM   Of course.

THE MADAM   You did say you wanted Father's Day?

SAM   Yes.

THE MADAM   It's a busy evening. I have Christmas going on in there, and Thanksgiving over there . . . Daughter's wedding upstairs. (*She underlines on her list*) Father's Day.

SAM   Yes. It's rather selfish . . . but I like it. I suppose most women ask for Mother's Day?

THE MADAM   I've never had a woman customer. Women don't seem to have any nostalgia for the Family . . . Now, how old was your wife?

SAM   Around twenty-five. . . . She chose early self-disposal many years ago.

THE MADAM   We have only one woman near that age, but she'll be your daughter. (*Checks her notes*) Age fourteen, you said.

SAM   Why can't she be my wife?

THE MADAM   She loves being a daughter, and she's very good. Just ignore the fact that she's pregnant.

SAM   Couldn't she be my wife? It would be wonderful to have a wife who's pregnant. Feel the baby kick. How far along is she?

THE MADAM   We've already made the assignment . . . Now, you said "chicken"?

SAM   Yes. I can smell it. Lovely.

THE MADAM   And the kitchen.

SAM   Yes. And messy, please. Florence was a terrible housekeeper.

THE MADAM   You'll have to get out by ten because a man is coming in at eleven who wants roast beef and an immaculate kitchen.

SAM   Oh, I'll be out.

THE MADAM   I must warn you that once in a while we're raided.

SAM   Raided?

THE MADAM   I've paid off the Captain. I let him come in once a week, free, and he stands around the piano with the biggest family I can get together, singing the old songs. Or I let him play at trains in the attic with one of the boys. But if one of those young punks on the squad breaks in, we're in trouble . . . If you hear the warning buzzer, take off your pants and start making love to your wife.

SAM   Does this happen often?

THE MADAM   No, but if they were ever to catch you and the family just sitting around here and eating and playing cards and that sort of thing, there'd be hell to pay.

SAM   (*Approaching a delicate subject*)   Uh . . . in most of the other Call Family Houses, they allow some . . . tenderness.

THE MADAM   (*Sternly*)   What do you mean?

SAM   They allow me to put my arm around my wife, if I feel like it . . . to touch her . . . to kiss.

THE MADAM   Well . . .

SAM   In an affectionate way.

THE MADAM   Well, all right. But be careful. These people find affection very difficult to handle. Many of them have never been kissed.

SAM   I'll be careful.

THE MADAM   (*Taking boxes from the* SON, *who has just entered*)   Now here are the presents you're bringing home from your trip.

SAM   Oh, yes. Thank you.

THE MADAM   What will you drink?

SAM   Oh, my God, at last. A double dry martini with a twist.

THE MADAM   (*Tears off sheet of instructions and gives them to the* SON *in the shadows*)   Now, remember, the Staff will not discuss war, bombs, air pollution, population, poverty, race, taxes or The System. Nor will it enter into discussions as to whether what we had before The System was freedom or chaos.
      (*She claps her hands for the set to change*)

SAM   Could I have a seven o'clock newscast? Cronkite . . . Huntley-Brinkley?

THE MADAM   (*As the inmates of the House move in the kitchen set in the shadows*)   All worn out long ago.

SAM   A newspaper then?

THE MADAM   We have only one left, and it's in terrible condition . . . Now, no more requests, or we'll never get you out of here on time.

> (*She claps her hands . . . and turns and leaves. The inmates of the Call Family House have been moving in the kitchen set. The lights come up full now, and we see it—an old-fashioned, cozy, messy kitchen. Checkered tablecloth, bowls slopping over with preparations, flour, dough, spice jars, vegetables, fruits, pots, pans, skillets, etc. If possible, an old-fashioned stained-glass lamp. The* DAUGHTER *comes in. She is around twenty-two, but dressed in a storybook outfit of a girl of fourteen, not unlike pictures of Alice in Wonderland. She is about five months pregnant. She is carrying a tray with* SAM'S *martini on it. There is something strange and eerie about her*)

DAUGHTER   Hello, Daddy. You're home early.

SAM   (*Looking at her*)   Well, yes . . . I guess I am.

DAUGHTER   That's nice. I always like it when Daddy comes home early. I'm sorry I wasn't at the front door to meet you. (SAM *stares at her*) What's the matter?

SAM   Nothing. You're very lovely, my dear.

DAUGHTER   I try to freshen up a little before you come home . . . Your martini. I hope you like it.

SAM   (*Can't take his eyes off her, charmed by her pregnancy*)   I know I will.

DAUGHTER   I think I made it too dry last night. See if it's all right.

SAM (*Tastes*) Mmmm. You always make it just right. Thank you. (*He moves to kiss her on the cheek. She moves away, confused and troubled*) It's all right. I have permission. Didn't she tell you?
>(*She allows herself to be kissed, but we can see her apprehension*)

DAUGHTER (*An excuse for moving away*) Let me take your jacket. (SAM *allows himself to be helped from his jacket*) Did you have a good day?
>(*During this, she hangs up* SAM's *coat and brings a smoking jacket, too big or too small, and some slippers*)

SAM Actually, I had a terrible day. The moving sidewalks broke down, and this evening the monorail stopped at the rush hour.

DAUGHTER (*As she helps him off with his shoes and puts the slippers on him*) Oh, what a shame. Poor Daddy.

SAM And the Union man caught me working today. I wasn't supposed to be working. But I went to the Library and took out this book I'm taping and went way back in the stacks . . . But he caught me . . .

DAUGHTER They shouldn't treat our nice daddy that way. (*He sits looking at her pregnant belly with appreciation. She gets nervous after a moment and jumps in with*) Did you bring me anything from your trip?

SAM Oh, yes . . . On the table there.

DAUGHTER (*Takes a box from the table*) Oh, it's lovely . . . I'll open it later in my room. You're always so thoughtful. You're the best father in the world.

SAM (*Still struck by her appealing pregnancy*) Why don't

you sit here, close to Daddy? (*She comes and sits, warily*) How old are you?

DAUGHTER Daddy! You know how old I am.

SAM Of course . . . How are we doing in school?

DAUGHTER I'm at the top of my class.

SAM (*Pats her*) Good . . . No problems we should discuss?

DAUGHTER (*Brightly*) No.

SAM You're sure?

DAUGHTER Yes.

SAM (*Disappointed*) I see . . . well . . . good . . . good.

DAUGHTER I was in the Pageant last week . . . Another girl and I sang a song.

SAM That's nice.

DAUGHTER Shall I sing it for you?

SAM Yes . . . please.

DAUGHTER (*Stands up and away from him, and sings very simply, but without feeling or understanding*)
Oh, little town of Bethlehem,
How still we see thee lie,
Above thy deep and dreamless sleep,
The silent stars go by.
Still in thy dark street shineth,
The Everlasting Light,
The hopes and fears of all the years
Are met in thee tonight.

SAM (*Like a kind father, he doesn't correct her and inform her it's Father's Day*) Very nice, dear . . . Very nice . . . Come and sit down. (*She sits again, warily. He looks fondly at her belly*) It's nice that you're going to have a baby . . . How far along are you? (*She looks coldly blank that he is intruding on her real life*) It might be my child, you know. I'm an IQSQC 240 and every week, I have to . . . you know . . . (*He makes a small move with his hand . . . He would like to put it on her belly, but he doesn't*) I had a child once, a personal child. One I conceived and brought up, till he was five. It was just during The Changeover, when The System was taking over. And when he was five, they came to give him his qualifying examination, and he didn't pass, and they took him away . . . You know, only so much space, air, food . . . Now, of course, you won't see your child. But in those days, we did . . . And it was terrible. Shortly after that, Florence . . .
　　(*He is troubled: he doesn't go on*)

DAUGHTER You mustn't be upset. It's Christmas.

SAM (*Gently*) Father's Day, dear . . . Father's Day.
　　(*The* SON *comes in, dressed in knickers and a sweater*)

SON Hello, Dad . . . Merry Christmas!

DAUGHTER (*Going to stand next to him, sotto voce*) Father's Day.
　　(SAM *looks at the* SON, *rises and stares at him*)

SON Did you have a good day, Dad?

DAUGHTER I've already asked that.

SON (*Notices the staring*) What's the matter, Dad?

SAM Don't you notice anything? (*The* SON *looks at the* DAUGHTER *as though to ask,* "*Do we have a zombie here?*" *To the* DAUGHTER) Don't you notice anything about . . . us? (*She looks mystified*) Any strong resemblance?

DAUGHTER Well, he's your son.

SAM But I think you *are* my son.

SON Well, of course. You want another drink, Dad? (*Upset, he moves to the sideboard*)

SAM Are you from around here?

DAUGHTER (*Warning*) Dad . . . Rules!

SAM But I used to look just like that. (*He comes closer to the* SON)

DAUGHTER (*Goes to one side and calls*) Mrs. Baldwin . . . We need you. (SAM *impulsively embraces the* SON, *who is disturbed*)

SON Hey, take it easy, Dad.

THE MADAM (*Comes to the edge of the kitchen*) Mr. Bradley, you know the rules.

SAM But you said I could show tenderness.

THE MADAM I know, but within limits.

SAM But I think this is really my son. So many women have had my children.

THE MADAM (*Kindly*) It's not an unusual reaction in a man your age. Just play along and enjoy it, and think what you want to think. (*Claps her hands sharply*) Now . . .

> (*As she leaves, she is met in the wings by the* WIFE, *dressed in a house dress with apron—middle-aged, comfortably, warmly glowing from the heat of the kitchen*)

WIFE (*Asking the* MADAM) Sam?

MADAM (*As she leaves*) Sam.

WIFE Sam! (*And she comes towards him*) Did you have a good day?

SAM Actually, I had a terrible day.

WIFE Dinner will be ready in a minute.

SAM I'm hungry as a bear.

WIFE But right now I need the help of a strong man. (*She holds out a jar*)

SAM Oh, yes. Let me. (*He takes it and opens it with ridiculous ease*) There.

WIFE What would we ever do without you!

SAM (*Modestly*) Oh.

WIFE When you're away, we're all a sixes and sevens around here. (*She goes on with her cooking preparations*) Ten times a day I turn to ask your advice. A house simply cannot manage without a man . . . Here. Here . . . Look at this. It broke and none of us can fix it. (*She hands him an eggbeater*) See what you can do with it.

SAM (*Looking at it*) I'll need a screwdriver. (*She produces one immediately from her apron*) Oh, thank you.
(*He proceeds to effect the very simple repair during the following*)

WIFE Have you been having a good chat with the children? They've been just sitting around here waiting to ask your advice on so many things.

SAM (*Has finished the repairs*) There.

WIFE Sam . . . Sam. You're a wonder. Look at that, children. You're a remarkable man, Sam. (*The* WIFE *hands the beater automatically to the* SON, *who automatically disposes of it*) You've got a button loose on your coat. Sister, fix your father's button.
(*The* DAUGHTER *has been getting the needle and thread before being told*)

SAM Oh, I didn't notice.

WIFE And there's a spot on the lapel. Gracious, you haven't been looking after yourself.

SAM (*Is delighted with the attentions*) Mmm . . . This all looks so good. (*He starts to poke his fingers into a bowl, and she raps them playfully*) Let me help, please.

WIFE All right. Finish setting the table.
(*She hands him knives and forks*)

SAM Oh, yes . . . I used to be very good at that . . . except I always forgot the napkins.
(*He can't take his eyes off the* SON)

WIFE (*Comes up to him playfully, changing the position of a knife*) Knives on the right . . . Good gracious, you've been away from home too long.

SAM Oh, yes.
(*He changes things. He keeps looking at the* SON, *who is sitting at the table*)

SON (*Nervously, to break the stare pointing at one of the boxes*) Is this for me?

SAM What? Oh, yes . . . No, not that one . . . This one.
(*And* SAM *picks another. They are all surprised that he has invented this new little twist to the game. They all laugh along with* SAM)

SON Thanks a lot. I'll open it in my room later.
(*He disposes of it*)

SAM (*Very courtly, to the* WIFE) And . . . this is for you.

WIFE Oh, thank you. That's so thoughtful of you.

SAM I spent hours looking for just the right thing. I hope you like it.

WIFE I know I will . . . I'll open it later . . . (*Cutely*) There seems to be one more present.

SAM (*He looks at them all*) For me? (*The* WIFE *makes a gesture he should take it.* SAM *picks it up. There is a card. He reads*) "To the best Dad in all the world . . ." . . . Isn't that nice . . . (*Playfully*) I wonder what it is? . . . It's not a tie . . . (*He shakes it*) It's not liquor . . . (*He smells it*) Cigars? . . . Let's see . . .
(*He starts to open it*)

WIFE Open it later . . . We're almost ready to eat.
(*The* DAUGHTER *takes it away from him, and sets it on the floor near the table. The* DAUGHTER *signals to the* SON. *He doesn't catch on for a moment. But then he does*)

SON Dad, can I have the car tonight?

SAM Well, uh . . .

DAUGHTER (*Into their routine*) You had it last night.

SON But only for an hour.

DAUGHTER (*Fighting back*) But you had it! I never get to use it.

SON Never! Ha-ha.

DAUGHTER Never! And I always have to buy the gas.

SON You buy the gas. What a laugh.

WIFE Children . . . children.

SAM (*A broad smile of appreciation on his face*) No . . . no . . . Let them . . . It's lovely.

SON I spend all my allowance on gas.

DAUGHTER You leave the tank absolutely empty. You must push the car into the garage.

WIFE That's enough, now! It's time for dinner. Sister, help serve.

SAM (*Embracing the* WIFE *from behind, fondly*) Oh, this is so good.

WIFE Careful now. You'll make me spill.

SAM (*Expansive*) I love the . . . (*Gestures, trying to include it all*) . . . the disorder of it all.
(SAM *holds a chair for the* WIFE)

WIFE You sit down. I'll be popping up and down every other minute.

SAM   Sit. At least while I say grace. (*The children look at each other, then they all sit and the* WIFE *instructs them by example what to do with their hands*) Dear Lord . . . we thank Thee for what is about to be placed before us. We thank Thee for so much . . . but especially for the beauty of the Family, the loving closeness . . . (*He is too moved to go on*) Amen. (*They all start to serve themselves, and* SAM *watches for a moment, then gets a sudden idea*) I'd like my father to be here. May I have my father?

WIFE (*To the* SON)   Go see if you can find Father.
      (*He goes*)

SAM   I want him to see me with my Family. I want him to sit at my table and eat my food.

THE MADAM (*At the edge of the set with the* SON)   Father is ten dollars extra.

SAM   I don't care. Bring him in.

THE MADAM   He's just finishing off next door . . . Now for God's sake, don't tell anyone outside we have a man over sixty in here.
      (*An old man comes in. He is just taking off his Santa Claus cap and beard. He remains dressed in his Santa Claus suit*)
      (SAM *gets up from the table and comes slowly towards him. It is clear that in spite of the fact that this is an absurd game, the symbolism of this old man reaches* SAM. *He is* FATHER. *The old man stands there, blinking his eyes, confused.* SAM *comes up to him and embraces him warmly, and holds him*)

SAM   Father, come in . . . Come in . . . I want you to sit at my table. To be with my Family. (*The* FATHER *starts to move to the table.* SAM, *going to the* SON, *who remains on the edge of the kitchen*) This is my son. (*The* FATHER *nods*) This *is* my son . . . I wonder if you know how rare it is for a father really to meet and know his own son. Look at us. Two peas in a pod . . . (*The* SON *begins to be upset. The* FATHER *nods*) *You* see it. *He* sees it. (*He turns to the others*)

WIFE   Come along. Eat . . . Eat. Sister, another dish for Father.

   (SAM, *standing next to* SON, *puts his arm around his shoulder, and stands next to him for them to compare*)

SAM   Look—same eyes, same mouth, same nose, same build . . . (*He draws him closer to his side and starts to ruffle his hair. The* SON, *genuinely upset at the prospect that he might have a father, pulls abruptly away from* SAM *and runs out*) Please . . . Please . . . (*Back to the others*) There is so much I want to say to him.

WIFE   He'll be back.

SAM   (*Returning to the table, to the* FATHER)   You noticed the likeness? (*The* FATHER, *doddering, nods*) There is so much advice I want to give him . . .

WIFE   Come along, now. Eat. Eat.

SAM   I'm sorry if I . . . What is the boy's name?

WIFE   Pass your plate, Sam. Come along, now.

SAM   Are you sure he'll be back?

WIFE   (*Serving him*)   Yes . . . yes . . .

SAM   (*Sitting at the table*)   How have you been, Father? (*The* FATHER *shrugs*) How do you like my Family? (*The* FATHER *looks at them and nods "very nice"*) Do you have a cigar, Father? . . . Would you smoke a cigar for me? (*Calls*) A cigar for my father! (THE MADAM *enters with a cigar box and offers it to the* FATHER. SAM *lights a cigar for the* FATHER, *who is obviously not a cigar smoker*) Do you remember when you gave me my first cigar when I was ten? You thought it would scare me off smoking . . . And I sat here at the table and later in the living room and smoked it to the end? (*Indicating the* DAUGHTER) She looks a little like Florence, doesn't she? Florence left me early in The System, Father. (*To the* WIFE) It doesn't bother you to have me talk about my first wife? It was long before you. No reason for you to be jealous of her. (*He rises*) I would like to play you a little bit of my first wife and me.

(*He moves to his coat*)

WIFE   Eat your dinner, Sam. You haven't eaten anything.

SAM   I'm editing our marriage. All marriages need editing. We had one of the first central taping systems.

WIFE   No, no. Now I draw the line. You can listen to her when you are away on your trips. But now you are home. Eat. Talk to us.

SAM   (*Sits down, looks at his Family with appreciation, then to the* FATHER) I like your cigar, Father . . . Do you remember in the library after Sunday dinner, you always smoked a cigar. You sat there and . . .
(*The memory suddenly touches him. He is silent*)

WIFE   (*Standing, moving beside where he is sitting*)   Now, let me help you. You must eat.
(SAM *suddenly puts his arm around her waist, as she stands near him, and draws her to him impulsively. He turns his head against her bosom. The* FATHER

27

and DAUGHTER *rise to protest that the rules are being broken*)

WIFE (*Gently, her arm around* SAM'*s shoulder*) No . . . no. It is allowed in this case. Permission has been given. (*She waves the* FATHER *and* DAUGHTER *away. They leave. When* SAM *is a bit more in control again*) So. Now we eat a little. A little wine.

SAM I'm sorry.

WIFE It's all right.

SAM It's all so nice . . . the messiness . . . the confusion . . . the smells . . . (*He sniffs her*) Nice, woman smells . . . I don't know . . . I don't know what's going to happen. First they took away my work, except for one day a week . . . Then The Family . . . I used to hate taking out the garbage . . . cutting the grass . . . painting the screens . . . Let me help you wash the dishes . . . please?

WIFE Later. If there's time.

SAM (*Remembering the time problem*) Oh, yes. (*Looking up at her seriously*) Why don't you come away and marry me?

WIFE But we *are* married.

SAM I mean really married.
(*A bell rings*)

THE MADAM (*From off, on her way in*) Time's up.
(*The* WIFE *turns on her heel and walks off, stripping off her black wig as she goes. She doesn't look back. Just leaves her place of work. The lights change*

abruptly from warm and cozy to "work light." THE
MADAM, *bringing him his coat and stripping him of
smoking jacket in the process, all very abrupt and
businesslike)*

THE MADAM   That's ten more for the Father, and a dollar
for the cigar.

SAM *(Confused by her abruptness)*   Yes, yes, of course.
He was very good. I would like to inquire about the boy.
I would like to—
   (Sound of loud buzzer)

THE MADAM   Oh, God. Take your pants off. Fast. *(She
starts to undo her blouse)* Take your pants off. The
police. (SAM *starting to comply, confused. He was getting the bum's rush, and now he must take his pants off)*
I told you . . . get them off. The police! *(She has her
blouse open, and is struggling with* SAM's *pants, as the*
CAPTAIN *comes in. The* CAPTAIN *is a man of fifty or so, in
uniform)* Oh, my God, it's just you . . . I've told them a
thousand times not to sound the alarm when it's you.

CAPTAIN   I'm sorry to disturb you.
   (SAM, *in utter confusion, continues to struggle to
take his pants off, and half grapples romantically
with* THE MADAM)

THE MADAM *(Brushing him off)*   Put your pants back on.
It's just the Captain. *(To the* CAPTAIN) This is not your
night.

CAPTAIN   I'm going to be away on Saturday.

THE MADAM   Everyone's busy. I can't get anyone to sing
around the piano with you.
   (SAM *is still confused and embarrassed. His pants*

have stuck down around his feet, and he is humili-
ated trying to get dressed while all this goes on)

CAPTAIN What about the trains . . . upstairs?

THE MADAM It's a busy night. I squeezed this man in.
I've got a roast beef dinner to serve here in half an
hour.

CAPTAIN The boy, who usually plays with the trains
with me?

THE MADAM He's gone.
(SAM *reacts, stopping at some awkward moment in
his dressing)*

CAPTAIN *My* son?

SAM (*Wants to protest that it's his son*) That boy . . .
that boy was—
(THE MADAM *pushes him aside and silences him)*

THE MADAM I'll take a boy away from another Family.

CAPTAIN But he was my son. He looked like me. He
talked like me . . .
(SAM *wants to butt in but only tries to maneuver
physically to where he can make his point)*

THE MADAM Look, I haven't got time to argue. Go to the
attic and I'll send up whoever I can find.

CAPTAIN (*Strongly*) I want my son!
(*And he leaves)*

THE MADAM (*To* SAM) Thanks a lot.

SAM But . . . but . . . the boy has gone?

30

THE MADAM Yes.

SAM (*Still struggling with his clothes—pants, coat, shoes*)
I wanted to give him something extra . . . If I come back
tomorrow night . . .

THE MADAM He's gone for good. And you won't be welcome at any Call Family House again.

SAM (*Pleading*) No! Please!

THE MADAM I made allowances for you to touch and
hold, but you went far beyond . . . It's very difficult to
train these people. I can't have them being upset like
that.

SAM Please . . . please . . . I couldn't live without
. . . this once a week, and my tapes of my marriage . . .
(*The inmates have started moving the kitchen off in
the shadows of the work lights*)

THE MADAM (*Very stern*) That was my best son . . . You
heard the Captain. He wants that boy. If he can't have
that boy to play trains with, he may let the house be
raided. All thanks to you. Now, get out . . .
(*And she starts to leave*)

SAM Please . . . Let me . . . let me . . . Listen, you're
very busy here. . . . You need another Father . . . I
could be a very good Father . . . I told you. I had a
child, my own child . . .
(*She has reached the shadows. He calls to her, one
last appeal. But she is gone.* SAM *gets himself together, sees the gift box at his feet. He turns away
from it, knowing that it is empty, takes a step or
two, straightening his coat. But who can resist opening a box? He steps back, picks it up, starts to un-*

31

wrap the paper, but stops, and tosses the whole thing down, and turns towards his cell, which has come onstage. He enters. SAM *stands for a few moments, contemplating what he will do. Finally, he pushes the lavender button)*

FEMALE VOICE   Review the valuables you may have with you. Those you wish to pass on to the Archives, place in the compartment which will now open.
   (*The compartment in the panel opens . . .* SAM *gathers his tapes, removes the slide of Florence, and puts them in the compartment)*

SAM   To whom it may concern. The way a man and woman lived before The System. Of historic interest . . . possibly. The voices are those of Sam and Florence Bradley.

FEMALE VOICE   Last words if you wish. At the sound of the beep, you may talk for approximately three minutes.
   (*Beep*)

SAM   (*Stands and says nothing for a long while . . . then*) I just don't like it here any more.

MALE VOICE   This is a warning. When you push the next button, the rest is irrevocable and automatic. (SAM *looks at the flashing "final" button, and then suddenly in a lunge pushes it. The lights change . . . A small panel opens revealing a pill and a glass of water)* The countdown has now begun. Swallow the pill and lie on the cot and wait.

SAM   (*Looks at the glass and pill, terrified. Suddenly he blurts out*)   A man can't live this way! He can't . . . He can't. . . . (*But he can't take the pill either. The slab-cot begin to slide out through an opening in the panel . . .* SAM *look at it, stunned . . . The slab then moves back in, and all the lights go out in the cell, and the compartment in which he has put his tape, snaps shut.* SAM *makes a lunge for his things, and tries to pry open the door*) Give me back my things . . . Please . . . I want my tapes. I can't live without my tapes! (*He looks around and senses that the cell has gone dead. No lights, no glowing buttons. He moves to the panel and pushes a few buttons. Nothing. Frantically he thinks of activating the cell by registering again*) Samuel Thomas Bradley . . . 1783.965.281 Stroke 6A IQSQC 240 . . . no address Employed by Central Library (*But he realizes it is doing no good. He is a non-person. He goes to the door, but it doesn't open*) Please, I want to leave now . . . I'd like to get out . . . Please . . . (*He shouts*) Somebody!

MALE VOICE We are sorry. You were warned the last step was irrevocable. Someone else is already breathing your air.

(*A clanging alarm bell starts . . .*)

The End

Double Solitaire

A bare stage . . . Except at stage left there is a round table with two chairs, and at stage right a round table with two chairs.

Slightly upstage center between the two tables, a screen or freestanding flat.

At the stage right table sits CHARLEY POTTER, *age forty-three. At the stage left table sits his attractive wife* BARBARA, *age forty-one.*

MRS. ELIZABETH POTTER, BARBARA'S *mother-in-law, comes from the shadows to* BARBARA'S *table. She is seventy-one, patrician . . . a lady who has missed a great deal in her life and knows it, but doesn't know just how it happened. She is a composed woman who speaks rather thoughtfully. A note of philosophic acceptance.*

MRS. POTTER   Ernest is having a perfectly wonderful time trying to decide what we should all do for our Fiftieth Anniversary. He's like a little boy with a birthday party to plan. He consults me, of course, but it will end up being all his way. He says it's an old tradition that the wedding is the bride's party and the Fiftieth Anniversary, the groom's. Of course he made it all up.

He's decided to ask the guests to bring pictures of *their* weddings, and he's going to have several projectors and show the pictures on the four walls of the banquet room . . . all at once. He says it's very modern . . . Perhaps it would be amusing to see the styles. But

I tell him many of the husbands and wives are dead, and some are divorced. Ernest says they needn't bring *their* pictures.

He's so proud of the ones he took at your wedding. We ran through them the other night, and they are lovely. Except, of course, for the ones of me. Ernest has always managed to get me at a poor angle. I tell him it's subconscious hostility. (*She smiles*) I say to him that good photographers weed out their poor pictures. But not Ernest. He shows them all. If he dies before I do, I'm going to get rid of at least half of them. (*After a moment*) Your mother wore such a pretty dress . . . The blue lace with the picture hat . . . And you were such a lovely bride . . . I was so happy that day, though you wouldn't think so from looking at Ernest's pictures of me . . . Happy for both of you, but most especially for Charley. And was he happy! You haven't seen the pictures for a long time, but wait till you see his face, looking at you with such adoration . . . You know, Barbara, you were only his third girl . . . He never would play the field. There was Betty when he was seven . . . Oh, yes, he started very young, head over heels in love. It's always had to be head over heels for Charley, or nothing . . . I used to say to him, when he couldn't get his special girl for a party, "Call up someone else. You don't have to marry the girl." But he wouldn't. He'd sit home and write the special girl a long love letter . . . I would have found it a great strain to have someone that devoted . . . Anyway, the sun rose and set with Betty . . . Then, at thirteen, it rose and set with Peggy . . . And then at nineteen, it rose and set with you . . . the best of them all. (*She pats* BARBARA's *arm, and looks at her a long moment*) Ernest's next idea for the party is that he and I should renew our marriage vows. He's in a great dither now trying to decide how to work in both the projections of the pictures and renewing the vows . . . I told him I wouldn't be able to go through the ring ceremony because of arthritis. (*She holds out her hands*) I haven't been able to get my wedding ring off for five years. I couldn't divorce him if I wanted to. (*She laughs*) And I've wanted to . . . often. In every marriage more than a week old, there are grounds for divorce. The trick is to find, and continue to find, grounds for marriage. (*An almost imperceptible look at* BARBARA) It's a romantic idea, this renewing the vows. But then men *are* the romantics, so full of nostalgia for the past they thought was so happy. I remember my youth as rather miserable. Ah youth, that happy time when I was so sad! . . . But they remember it as so happy . . . I imagine it has something to do with their sex drive. That's so important to them. I remember my fifties as being my happiest years. The children were grown, there were grandchildren whom I could cuddle for a few minutes and then thrust back into their mothers' aching arms. (*She laughs*) Another of Ernest's romantic ideas has always been to move to the country, to a farm. Get away from it all. The simple life. Family picnics under the spreading maple trees. Of course he forgets the mosquitoes. Men always forget the mosquitoes . . . I do hope they've removed Thoreau from school reading lists. The image of that dreadful shack at Walden has made more men unhappy and wrecked more marriages. (*A long moment*) One final thing . . . Ernest is going to talk to Charley and suggest that you and he stand up with us and renew your marriage vows too. (*She looks at* BARBARA *for a long moment*) We renewed our vows on our twenty-fifth. Perhaps it helped, because here we are . . . And we have a good life. I have my garden, though I can't work in it as much as I used to. And there's the church . . . And I read a good deal.

And Ernest and I play cards. I always hated cards, but he finally persuaded me . . . We play double solitaire . . . You know, each one lays out his own deck, but you put the aces in the center as they come up, and each builds on them . . . The play of the cards is lively. We have little jokes about the game . . . I slap his hand when he plays on a card I was about to build on. And we laugh. And he teases me . . . It gives us something to do together. And I have my poetry readings. I'm reading at The Club next Tuesday if you're free . . . Two-thirty. (*She recites, very simply*)

All, all of a piece throughout.
Thy chase had a beast in view.
Thy wars brought nothing about.
Thy lovers were all untrue.
'Tis well when old age is out,
And time to begin anew.

(*After a moment, as she draws on a glove*)
Not exactly what the ladies want to hear. But I find those lines strangely comforting . . . There'll be coffee and sandwiches after. Rather better than you usually get at such affairs.

She reaches out and puts her hand on BARBARA'*s arm and looks at her a moment and smiles. She moves back into the shadows.* BARBARA *remains at her table. As* MRS. POTTER *walks into the shadows, slides of a wedding and wedding party start to show on the screen or flat in the center. And* ERNEST POTTER, *age seventy-five, enters. He is a gentleman of the old school, full of warm charm. Very handsome, and, for his age, jaunty and youthful in spirit*)

40

MR. POTTER   When I took that one, I was standing in the middle of your mother's flower bed. I got hell for it, but the shot was worth it. (*A shot or two of* BARBARA *and* CHARLEY *in the garden*) You can make a choice of those you might want to show at the party and keep them all. I always meant for Barbara and you to have them . . . They've stood up very well for twenty-two years. (*A picture of* MRS. POTTER. *Nothing too poor, but just not very good*) Not very good of your mother. But then, she doesn't take a good picture. I've tried my damnedest over the years . . . She's a beautiful woman, too . . . There's a couple along here I particularly want you to see.

CHARLEY   (*Turns away, obviously disturbed and saddened a bit by the pictures*)   I'll look at them later, Dad. Thanks.

MR. POTTER   I showed them to Peter the other day when he was over. He was very interested in them. Maybe you'd like to show them to Mary, too. It's nice for children to be able to see their parents when they . . . uh . . . well . . . as they were then.

CHARLEY   Yes.
         (*The pictures stop for the time being*)

MR. POTTER   Now, Charley, see how this fits in with your plans for the party. I thought the first part of the evening we'd have festivities. There are going to be a lot of people who haven't seen each other for a long time, and they'll want to say hello and have a drink.

CHARLEY   There's a small room off the main room at the hotel, and we'll have a bar set up there, and a little music.

MR. POTTER   Then I thought we'd have dinner, and then right after dinner, your mother and I have decided we'd like to renew our marriage vows. We did it on our twenty-fifth, you remember.

CHARLEY   That's a nice idea, Dad.

MR. POTTER   And then after that, more festivities, and the slides and pictures.

CHARLEY   Maybe the vows should be before dinner.

MR. POTTER   I thought of that, but there'll be a lot of drinking then, and I thought maybe after dinner the food would have absorbed some of the champagne. We could do it before the dessert and champagne.

CHARLEY   Or you could do it before everything, so everything after would be party, the way it was fifty years ago.

MR. POTTER   Well, let's turn it over in our minds. Your mother will have some very definite ideas about it, but if you and I stick together, we might prevail. She had it all her way the first time. (*Change of mood*) Now, Charley, I tell you what your mother and I would like. What would make our anniversary for us. It wouldn't cost you a penny . . . Your mother and I would like you and Barbara to stand up and renew your marriage vows along with us. (CHARLIE'*s smile sets*) It would give us great pleasure, old man.

   (CHARLEY'*s mouth opens, but for a moment nothing happens. Then he licks his lips and goes on*)

CHARLEY   I . . . uh . . . well . . . This is your party, Dad . . . and . . .

MR. POTTER   Your mother has talked to Barbara about it, and you can discuss it, but I can't tell you what it would mean to us.

CHARLEY   Dad, it's . . . well, we'll think about it.

MR. POTTER   It would be good for you, too, Charley . . . It helped your mother and me on our twenty-fifth. There's something reaffirming about the ritual . . . to stand in the presence of God and your friends and your family and say . . . "To have and to hold . . . in sickness and in health . . . for better or for worse . . ."

CHARLEY   Dad, you know neither Barbara nor I are very religious any more . . . There would be a certain . . . hypocrisy.

MR. POTTER   I don't look upon it as a religious ceremony, Charley. It's . . . I don't know. There's something about standing up there, in the face of all the unhappy marriages . . . the divorces . . . the whole mess out there, to stand up there and say, "We made it!"

CHARLEY   We'll think about it, Dad.

MR. POTTER   Maybe while you're going through the ceremony, we could flash one of the pictures on the wall. (*He flips through a couple of shots, and ends with a close shot of* CHARLEY *and* BARBARA, *embracing. Pantomime of* CHARLEY *shutting off the projector*)

CHARLEY (*Smiling at his dad's efforts to show the films*) Later, Dad . . . I'd like to look at them later on. Slowly. You know?

MR. POTTER (*After a moment*) Charley?

43

CHARLEY Yes, Dad?

MR. POTTER Your mother's worried about you.

CHARLEY (*Smiling*) Why, Dad?

MR. POTTER She's a very wise woman. She senses something, and I think she just may be right.

CHARLEY About what?

MR. POTTER Charley, you're only going through what every couple in the world has gone through.

CHARLEY Come on now, Dad . . .

MR. POTTER Damn it, Charley, I didn't give you much advice about things, women and sex and all that, when you were growing up. I assumed you were learning it some place . . . But now, Charley, what the hell's the use of what I know and have learned if it can't help you? . . . They used to call them The Dangerous Years . . . Hell, every year of marriage can be dangerous if you want to make it that way. If you're not committed. But if you're committed, you get by them, by them all. You just bite the nail and hang on.

CHARLEY Dad—

MR. POTTER —Renew your vows, Charley! I put great store by form and routine and ritual. They sound dull, but they carry you along. A lot of times in my life, I haven't felt like doing a thing. I didn't care if school kept or not. But I went ahead and did whatever I was supposed to do. And often I'd get a surprise. Halfway through, there suddenly was some feeling. Presents I'd give your mother. Hell, sometimes it starts out as a perfunctory note from my secretary: "Don't forget your wife's birthday." And I've got no interest in it. And very little love for her on that particular day . . . And then I make the effort and don't just send my secretary out for something. And before I've finished selecting the present, I can't wait to get home and give it to your mother. And at that moment I love her.

CHARLEY You're an old campaigner, Pop. An old soldier.

MR. POTTER Bring home some flowers unexpectedly, for no reason at all. Whisk her away on a trip on the spur of the moment . . . Your mother keeps telling me, "You can't play the show over again." But it never hurts to try. (*A better idea*) Take her for a night to a hotel here in your own city. There's something very exciting about that.

CHARLEY (*Smiles*) Did you do all those things, Dad?

MR. POTTER (*The old sport*) Most of them. And a few more. Your mother wouldn't go for the hotel. She said it was ridiculous for us to go to a hotel when we had our own apartment. Your mother sometimes lacks the light touch. That's not meant as a criticism. Just an observation. She's a fine woman . . . Look, Charley, someday someone's going to come up with a better set-up. They haven't yet. So the answer is accept the situation and find your own way to make it work . . . And don't ask too many questions . . . And I've got to tell you, old man, it gets worse . . . But a man doesn't whine. A dog whines. But a man doesn't whine . . . Wait till she goes through The Change. Women are impossible in that period. And at least for your mother, it was the end of . . . (*He makes a gesture, knowing* CHARLEY *will understand*) I mean, finished! Without any

45

"I'm sorry's" or "What are you going to do?" . . . And the thing is so damned delicate. Naturally you don't bring it out in the open and discuss it. You just let it ride. Oh, a more aggressive man might have made a big issue of it and blown the marriage sky-high, made the wife think she was some kind of monster. I mean, I didn't think very pretty thoughts when I finally realized what had happened without any mention of *my* problem. But I didn't say anything to her. You don't say everything you think . . . And I'm still a vigorous man in that area. (*He smiles jauntily*) So you should be, too. They say it's a matter of inheritance.

CHARLEY (*Amused at the old fox*)   I look upon that as my most valuable inheritance, Dad.

MR. POTTER   Of course I don't do anything about it, out of respect for your mother, who is a fine woman. I know she needn't have known. But *I* would have known. I hear about all these people sleeping around, and I ask myself, "If I had gone to bed with this or that woman . . ." And I've had the opportunity . . .

CHARLEY   I'm sure you have, Dad. You're a charming man.

MR. POTTER   You pulling my leg?

CHARLEY   No. I mean it.

MR. POTTER   Well, some women have found me attractive. And on trips, in the course of my business, sometimes it almost seemed harmless. But your mother is a fine, clean woman, and I couldn't have come back to her if I'd done that. (*He had said this with great force, as though someone had been arguing with him*) Now, your Uncle Philip . . . He's played fast and loose with woman after woman. *Now* where is he? No children. No family. Lolling away his life on a beach down in Florida. Nothing accomplished. We wouldn't let him bring his women to the house because of the effect it might have on you and Ruth when you were children . . . Perfectly beautiful women, laughing all the time . . .

CHARLEY   I was always fond of Uncle Philip.

MR. POTTER   Well, you were too young to know the truth . . . I don't know how he does it. Where he gets his money . . . But he'll come whining in the end for a handout. Or he'll be lonely. *Something* will happen to him. It's *got* to! (*He has said this with determination. The man just can't get away with it!* . . . *and then he relaxes*) So, Charley, you coast . . . as I said. Just be happy you can get from one end of the week to the next. Join some clubs. Find some committees. All those committees I'm on. Scenic Preservation . . . Museum of Natural History . . . Boys' Club . . . You don't think I'm really interested in all those things? . . . But they have meetings . . . And I've got my hobbies . . . Shot an eighty-six yesterday . . . And my cameras. You started me on that interest, Charley. Saved my life . . . Then there's the Board of Education . . . YMCA . . . We go to the movies at least once a week, and one night in my darkroom . . . Time passes. (*He looks at* CHARLEY *for a moment, then gets up, preparing to leave*) When this anniversary business is over, let's us go off fishing together. Get a boat, and go out in the middle of a lake and get to know each other.

CHARLEY   That's a good idea, Dad.

MR. POTTER (*Puts his hand on* CHARLEY'S *shoulder*) Just remember . . . Bite on the nail.

(*He pats his son and moves off into the shadows. From the shadows comes* SYLVIA, *an extremely stylish woman around forty. She talks as she moves to* BARBARA'S *table*)

SYLVIA I wouldn't marry again for a million dollars. I was a very boring wife. I came to know exactly what I was going to say on every occasion and said it . . . Oh, I read all the books on how to be a thousand different women for your husband . . . On one occasion I even suggested an innovation or two in our sex lives, which had the unfortunate effect of blocking him completely for two weeks. So I finally persuaded him to divorce me (sans alimony, of course. I have my own shop, and I wasn't going to fleece him because I was a frumpy bore). I lost ten pounds and immediately became more attractive and interesting . . . at least to myself.

"Don't you get lonely?" they ask me. Who has time to be lonely? "Who do you see?" My God, I see their husbands. Not my friends' husbands, of course. I use some discretion. And it's not all sex, or even mostly . . . I find that every man has enough interesting happen to him in a week to fill one evening's conversation.

Mondays I see this movie bug. He has to sit near the screen, and his wife has to sit far back. For years they compromised and sat in the middle and spoiled it for both of them. Also, she is an easy weeper and cries at almost everything, which annoys him and makes him feel insensitive. And he laughs easily, which makes her feel she has no sense of humor . . . So . . . Tuesdays I see this man who loves games . . . particularly Scrabble. His wife thinks games are frivolous, and besides

she can't spell . . . Wednesday is matinee day, and
there's this sweet older man. He doesn't like to sit up
late, so we have an early dinner after the matinee and
I go home and get to bed early. A-lone. He's just had
a heart attack, so that's why I'm free today . . . Thurs-
days I have lunch with this nice homosexual boy. That
takes care of my mothering instincts . . . Thursday
nights there's this man who likes to come and sit in my
neat, pretty, attractive apartment . . . His sexual rela-
tions with his wife are marvelous, but she's a slob
about her house. So he just comes and sits in my apartment and we talk. Each time he comes, he walks
through my rooms and looks at them, shaking his head
. . . Friday and Saturday nights are heavy date nights
. . . Sundays I have *The New York Times*, and I do my
other reading to keep up with the various interests of
my dates . . . *Scientific American* . . . *Art News* . . .
Cahiers du Cinéma . . . *Fortune* . . . *Sports Illus-
trated* . . .

Now and then, of course, one of them asks me to
marry him. A kind of conditioned reflex learned at
Mother's knee . . . to make an honest woman of me. I
find they usually ask at just about the time they're
getting tired of making an effort. They're ready to take
me for better or worse and for granted . . .

I much prefer to be a visitor in a person's life. I get
treated with much more consideration.

Of course it gets lonely on Mother's Day and Christmas and other tribal times when families rush off to
graduations and weddings, Bar Mitzvahs and circum-
cisions . . . But what the hell. I have a little warm dog
who sleeps in my bed . . . when no one else is there,
naturally. Some men are really thrown by having a
dog stand there watching them. (*She laughs*) They say

49

I'll be lonely when I'm old . . . Well, I can always take a few pills or cut my throat . . . I mean, life was meant to be lived, not just endured.

(*And she drifts off into the shadows. As she leaves,* GEORGE *comes down to* CHARLEY . . . GEORGE *is a man in his late forties, a man of great experience, rough-hewn, warm and charming. His most characteristic attitude towards things is expressed by laughing and shaking his head sadly at the same time . . . muttering, "Sad . . . Sad." He is paternal towards* CHARLEY *in a nice way*)

CHARLEY (*Intense*) My father expected me to say right out, "Sure, great." And I opened my damned mouth to say it, and nothing came out. And that's all I've been able to think about since.

GEORGE (*Laughs*) God, it's sad.

CHARLEY I haven't discussed it with Barbara. She hasn't discussed it with me. We each know the other one's been asked, but neither of us is saying anything. (GEORGE *laughs. This sort of perverse situation delights him*) What I'm talking about is me sitting there with my mouth open and nothing coming out. Like finding yourself unable to function with a girl when you want to, or think you want to. You have every intention, but something inside you that knows you a lot better shouts, "You're a damned liar." And doesn't let you do what you think you want to do. And then you start to sweat and ask questions . . . like "If you can't feel that way about her, what are you doing married to her?" It's been a rough few days.

GEORGE (*Asking the obvious but inappropriate question*) So, what are you going to do, get a divorce? (CHARLEY *looks at him as though he were crazy*) Well, you can't just sit there and say, "It shouldn't be this way."

CHARLEY (*Loud*)   It *shouldn't* be this way!
  (*Then he smiles*)

GEORGE   You know, Charley, your reaction to things like this always reminds me of a guy with a football. He starts running down the field, and he suddenly sees a lot of tacklers in the way. He says to himself, "God damn it, they shouldn't be there. According to The Book, the interference should have taken them out." You get mad and run right into the tacklers and get thrown for a loss. You've got to learn to . . . improvise.

CHARLEY   George, how the hell have we been friends all these years? You think I'm a sentimental dope . . . naive . . .

GEORGE   And you think I'm a cynical old bastard.

CHARLEY   Sometimes I've envied you your cynicism.

GEORGE   Sometimes I've envied you your . . . what? . . . your ridiculous battle with the inevitable . . . I'm not cynical. Just seven years older than you. Look down and you'll see my footprints in the sand . . . slightly bloody.

CHARLEY (*Smiles*)   Barbara hates for me to spend time with you. She says you give me wild ideas. She says I always come home restless and grind my teeth in my sleep. (*Back to his problem*) Damn it, George, the thing itself, renewing the vows, is not that important, but it's set up a whole chain of reactions. By realizing I don't feel the way I should to stand up there with deep commitment and conviction, I suddenly got a terrible sense of the absence of that feeling . . . in my life. And I was, and am, scared to death.

GEORGE (*Be reasonable*) Well, Charley . . .

CHARLEY I know. But it suddenly made me hungry for it. Desperately hungry for that intensity.

GEORGE I'll have my book finished in a week or so and turn it over for your blue pencil. That'll keep you busy and take your mind off it.

CHARLEY I don't seem to want to take my mind off it. It's made me put my mind *to* it. (*Suddenly intense*) Christ, George. . . . do you know there's nothing I'd die for. (GEORGE *just looks at him, taken aback a little, and touched by the flat-out nature of the statement*) It's an overblown way of putting it. But these few days have made me wonder, "Jesus, what do I feel strongly about?" I whip up some passing superficial enthusiasm. But not enough to march or even sign my name to a protest . . . My life seems to be spent in discussing the day's news and the latest movies . . . Entirely superficial. God, you're the only one I ever talk to like this. The rest of my friends would be embarrassed. And I don't know anything about where they *really* live . . . I used to talk to Barbara, but . . .
  (*He shrugs*)

GEORGE Yes, I know. Frighten her to death. The dark side of a husband's soul is too threatening for a wife to take seriously . . . I told Doris once about a kind of homosexual dream I had had. It had bothered the hell out of me for days, and I wanted to talk about it to someone. She laughed and said, "You,

George! Ha-ha." . . . And the next time we were together, she said, "Well, this is better than little boys, isn't
it?"

CHARLEY (*Smiles and shakes his head*) Suddenly I'm ex-
amining everything I do and feel, and so much of it
seems too damned pointless. I mean, yesterday I'm up
there making out the monthly checks, and I found myself stopping and asking, "Which of these damned things
I'm paying for do I really care about?" . . . and I went
through an unconscious withdrawal into a kind of
fantasy. I wanted the house to burn down. Or maybe
I wanted my whole life to burn down . . . And then I'd
sit in a bare white-walled room, and anything or anyone who wanted "in" to that room or my life would
have to pass the most rigorous test for meaningfulness
. . . And I would want to start in that room with a
woman. Because I'm no good as a swinging single
. . . A woman about whom I could feel and continue
to feel with such intensity that my whole life would
take on meaning . . . Because that's the way it was
when Barbara first came into my room . . . I was
nothing . . . (*He stops . . . then after a moment, starts
to smile*) Then, of course, I start coming to. I realize that
she would need clothes, and that I'm easily bored in
one room . . . and we'd want children . . . and . . . and
. . . and . . . And I join the human race.

GEORGE You want too much, Charley (*Then in a lighter
tone*) Get an accountant to make out your checks.

CHARLEY (*Smiles*) Remove myself from all points of
contact with my life, the points that let me know what I
feel . . . My checkbook . . . sex. Someone else to pay

the bills. Someone else or me-but-not-really-me to sleep with my wife . . . Cool . . . That would scare the Bejesus out of me, George. I sense something about myself, that I could be the damnedest most detached person, and I could freeze to death somewhere out there in the cool world, without this connection with life through my feelings for someone . . . That's why this blandness terrifies me. I feel my spiritual temperature dropping, and I get scared, and I reach out desperately for some saving intensity and itimacy. (*He pauses for a moment . . . then . . .*) Barbara and I achieve this intensity and intimacy sometimes in sex. There can be nothing, and then . . . something. Primitive. A connection and intensity. And it dissipates this blandness and emptiness for a while . . . It used to be a joke, when I was in college. I always fell in love with anyone I went to bed with. Fortunately, it still works . . . even when all the other lines of intimacy and communication are blocked.

GEORGE   I have my work. Maybe that's what I'd die for.

CHARLEY   You're lucky. Much as I enjoy editing you and some of my other authors, it's not that meaningful to me. And my own writing—I'm afraid by being cowardly about my commitment to that years ago, it's no longer that fulfilling or urgent . . . Two roads diverged in a yellow wood . . . and I . . . I didn't take either one of them, but slogged into the middle of the woods, trying to keep an eye on both roads, hoping they might eventually come together . . . Son of a bitch, George, *what* do you do? . . . My father sensed I was upset. He suggested I bring home some flowers unexpectedly. (*They both smile at this*) Or take her to a hotel right here in New York, where we have our apartment. He says that's very sexy.

GEORGE I never tried that one. I did the flowers, of course, and then a slightly too-expensive present for no reason at all . . . It didn't have the desired effect. Doris was sure I'd been cheating on her.

CHARLEY Had you?

GEORGE Not yet. I was going through the same period you're going through now. Depressed as hell, scared because I didn't feel "that way" about her, and trying to rediscover it . . . Doris and I hadn't been dancing for ten years, and I took her dancing . . . After the first set, her feet began to hurt and my bursitis was getting me in the right arm, and so we huddled in the corner by the candlelight, and ordered champange, which I hate, and tried to be romantic for a while . . . Then we both felt foolish and talked about the children.

CHARLEY (*Smiles*) I did something . . . When I came back from the Service, I'd gotten into the habit of wearing my skivvies, my underwear, to bed . . . One time, I started wearing pajamas instead . . . just the tops. And I started shaving before going to bed. And I cleared all the magazines from my night table, and I just lay there waiting for her as she came out of the bathroom.

GEORGE (*Laughs*) Jesus.

CHARLEY It terrified her. She began to take longer and longer before she came out. And she took to wearing older and older nightgowns . . . and she finally came to bed with a ratty old tennis sweater over everything . . . I went back to wearing my skivvies.

GEORGE How did the kidnapping bit work out? (CHARLEY *looks at him*) Dragging her off on the spur of the moment to some romantic weekend spot. (CHARLEY

looks at him, pained and amused) You don't think I did
that? You think I'm some unfeeling monster? We all do
that. The whole damned thing is a cliché. That's what
makes art and literature possible . . . Where'd you take
her?

CHARLEY I've got this thing for beaches. We were together first on a beach at Ipswich.

GEORGE I took Doris to Pennsylvania—Bucks County.
No luggage, no nothing. I just grabbed her one summer evening, shoved her in the car, and went . . . We
had to stop in the village down there to get a bathrobe,
because she said what if the john were down the hall?
And while we were buying the bathrobe, we got a
sweater and skirt because it was turning chilly, and
under the circumstances I wanted her to be happy
. . . Anyway . . . the whole damned thing turned into
a shopping expedition. You see, Charley, it's to laugh.

CHARLEY Yeah.

GEORGE You think I'm cynical, my women, my girls.
The way I carry on . . . I wasn't cynical when I married Doris. I was sick with love for her. Do you imagine
I'd have even thought of laying a hand on another girl?
. . . Hell no . . . And that was beautiful . . . But, man,
you can't keep it up, and I tried. And she tried . . . So,
you go underground, keep your own confidence, be
careful, discreet . . . and . . . a little sad. If you don't,
you get a lot of divorces, which makes everyone unhappy . . . Marriage isn't long for this world, Charley.
The women are saying they're fed up with it. The men
will finally get honest and say they don't like it. The
kids won't have it. They're getting rid of all that bull-
shit. My youngest son tells me, "We're reexamining all

your institutions to see if they suit us." I can't wait for them to hit marriage . . . We're transitional figures, Charley. And it's rough to be a transitional figure.

CHARLEY   I *like* marriage. I thought. I hate the old bastard for disturbing my sleep . . .

GEORGE   (*After a moment*)   Charley, we've asked each other a lot of dirty questions over the years. Let me ask you one now. Would you feel this . . . hypocrisy if you were standing up there at this make-believe altar with Maria? (CHARLEY *smiles at him*) Have you been in touch with her?

CHARLEY   Not for a long time. We wrote for a while after I came back from California. Then . . .

GEORGE   She just got divorced.

CHARLEY (*Smiles*)   Yeah. I heard about it. It's been coming for a long time.

GEORGE   You "heard" about it . . . So my question stands. If I ever saw a man in love, you were in love with Maria. You came back from California raving about her poetry, this beautiful new poet . . . I don't think anyone was deceived. (CHARLEY *smiles*) Which came first? Your father's suggestion about renewing your vows, or your hearing of Maria's divorce?

CHARLEY   My father on Monday . . . Maria on Wednesday.

GEORGE   I would say she timed her divorce with a total lack of consideration for you.

CHARLEY   My thing with Maria was more or less a one-way street. I was crazy about her . . . But she was,

oh . . . It was hard to tell how she felt about me really.
She was having a rough time with her husband . . .
(*Shrugs*) But you're right. That's part of the last few
days. The way I felt when I heard that . . . I walked
the streets like a caged tiger . . . I tell you those two
things coming together . . . I worked out a dozen
schemes to take me to California. Young authors we
publish who need checking on. Wild-goose chases to
sell another of my stories to the movies. I wrote Maria
a dozen letters in my mind. I was alive . . . I didn't have
a drink all day. I didn't need one. At the end of the day
I found myself in a flowershop ordering her favorite
flowers. I wrote out five different messages to go with
them . . . And then I finally said, "You can't go this
route." . . . And I picked out some other flowers and
took them home to Barbara.

GEORGE (*Shakes his head and smiles sadly*) God . . .

CHARLEY We both got a little high . . . and . . . we had
a good time . . . And just before I fell asleep, she said,
"Charley, do you have to be high to make love to me?"
(GEORGE *shakes his head*) I copped out by pretending to
be asleep. But I didn't sleep that night, thinking about
that . . . The next night I didn't have a drink before
dinner or after dinner. And I was very conspicuous
about not having one. And I started to make love to her
. . . as a kind of answer . . . But she was tired . . . So
. . . it isn't true . . . really.
  (*But he still wonders*)

GEORGE (*After a moment*) I understand Maria's on her
way to London . . . going to stop off in New York to
see shows . . . and old friends.
  (*He looks at* CHARLEY)

CHARLEY (*Smiles . . . shakes his head*) No.

GEORGE I've heard that from alcoholics and chain-smok-
ers.

CHARLEY No. It took me three months to stop thinking
about her the last time . . . I had to stop writing her,
ask her to stop writing me . . . I thought I could go on
pouring out my heart to her in letters and still keep on
with Barbara . . . on another level . . . Again, keeping
my eye on two roads. I shocked myself one morning,
writing an adoring letter to Maria after having made
love to Barbara the night before . . . I felt like that man,
you remember, your friend . . . the man whose wife
caught him in bed with another woman, and he jumped
up stark naked yelling, "It's not me. It's not me."
(*He smiles at the picture . . . then*) But it *was* me
. . . sleeping with Barbara and writing the letters to
Maria. And I desperately longed to be just one "me."
So I quit writing.

GEORGE (*Smiling*) And immediately she vanished from
your mind.

CHARLEY How the hell do you keep your feelings straight
with your various girls?

GEORGE The difference is I'm not in love with any of
them. I don't want to write letters of undying love to
any of them. I don't seem to have your need to adore.
(*There is a note of sadness in all this*) I'm my own man,
in sickness and in health, for better or for worse . . . till
death do part me from myself. (*After a moment*) You
want too much, Charley . . . What right have you got
to have things simple?

CHARLEY (*Smiling, acknowledging*) The motto of my family is *Dum spiro, spero* . . . While I breathe, I hope . . . (*Then seriously*) I asked Barbara to go to the Bahamas with me for a quick week . . . one of the outer islands . . . to get away from it all.

GEORGE Once more onto the beach, dear friend.
(*He shakes his head*)

CHARLEY She said she was too busy with the preparations for the party.

GEORGE Perhaps just as well . . . I have friends who wrangled along in the city, always with the illusion that if they could get away from the clutter of their lives and be alone in the country, things would be better for them . . . When their kids left home, they took to the woods, and looked at each other across the uncluttered space and promptly got a divorce . . . I try to confront my illusions as rarely as possible.

CHARLEY She'd go if I insisted.
(*They look at each other a long moment . . . the unstated statement . . . "Why haven't I insisted?"*)

GEORGE (*Puts his hand on* CHARLEY'*s shoulder . . .*) Keep breathing, Charley.
(*He moves off into the shadows.* CHARLEY *runs a few slides of the wedding. At about the third slide,* PETER, *age twenty-two, appears in the shadows, looking at the slides. He is very youthful and attractive . . . Wears sweater, jeans, sneakers . . .*)

PETER Dad?

CHARLEY Oh, yes, Peter.

PETER You wanted to talk over my plans.

60

CHARLEY Yes. Come in.
(PETER *comes to his father and kisses him on the cheek*)

CHARLEY You've seen these, I think.

PETER Yes. Grandfather showed them to me. (*They look at two or three more*) They're nice. (*It is obvious he thinks them rather painful, but he feels he has to say something*) The color has stood up very well.

CHARLEY You've heard your grandfather's plan. The guests to show pictures of their weddings on all four walls simultaneously.

PETER (*Smiles*) Melinda and I took him to The Electric Circus. That's probably where he got the idea.

CHARLEY (*Stops the projector*) I'm surprised he hasn't persuaded you and Melinda to get married as part of the Festivities. (PETER *smiles a little uncomfortably*) You mean that gracious, charming old couple walking hand in hand into the Sunset doesn't persuade you of the joys of matrimony? (PETER *smiles again*) Tell me your plans.

PETER Well, I've told you I've got this short film I made . . . about three minutes. I brought it to show you.

CHARLEY Good.

PETER Melinda and I thought we'd go abroad with it. Try to show it around at some of the small film festivals . . . and just wander around Europe.

CHARLEY Sounds great.

PETER After that, well, I just want to make films and be with Melinda . . . I've been getting along on fifty bucks a week, and I can always pick that up anyplace. And

Melinda speaks perfect Italian and French, and she can always work as a tutor . . . And that's all we need . . . If we don't get involved with things.

CHARLEY (*Smiles*) Lots of luck.

PETER Well, I mean, what's the point of it?

CHARLEY Somehow things accumulate without your noticing.

PETER (*Very serious*) We always want to keep it very, you know, very simple. You've seen how we live now. A bed, our books and records.

CHARLEY You know, your mother dreads it when I go to visit you and Melinda. I get painfully nostalgic for all that . . . and I come home with a tremendous desire to simplify my life. I start throwing everything away . . . I know it's none of my business, but what about children?

PETER (*Knew this would come up*) No.

CHARLEY I sense a lot of thinking behind that "No."

PETER (*Gestures with his hands . . . he is uncomfortable*) We've talked a lot about it . . . I guess we're being selfish, but we don't want to have children unless we're married, and we don't want to be married, that is, legally . . . to be tied down. (*Tries another way of putting it*) I mean, I love coming home to Melinda now. You'll see it in the film . . . We've promised each other that if either of us, well, stops feeling that way . . . (*In his difficulty, he gets direct and specific and slightly accusing*) I don't know . . . I just don't ever want to have to swill a pitcher of martinis before I come home to my wife. (*He looks at his father a moment, embarrassed at the accusing tone*) I don't mean you. But I've seen it.

CHARLEY Don't exclude me. There have been times. Maybe not a pitcher, but a few.

PETER (*Worked up, as though he were being attacked*) It's just not going to happen to us! . . . I can't imagine, we can't imagine . . . I mean, my feeling for Melinda has made all the difference in my life. You saw it. I was nothing before she came along. All right, so they tell us it can't last. We don't believe that. We believe we have something quite special, and *if we watch it* . . . But, if it doesn't last, neither of us can imagine living without that . . . (*He searches for the word "intense" but his tension expresses it*) . . . feeling for *someone*. We've promised each other . . . (*He half-kiddingly raises his hand to take an oath*) To love, or . . .
     (*He shrugs*)

CHARLEY "Split?" (PETER *acknowledges the word is right*) Rocks split . . . Wood splits . . . People tear, and usually rather painfully. I'm sorry to sound so wise . . . to be so sententious. It comes with the role . . . You want absolute freedom, Peter. I'm not so sure there is such a thing, or even if it's entirely desirable. You know, commitments have their surprising rewards.

PETER We're committed to each other now. We understand that.

CHARLEY I don't want to embarrass you, but your mother and I never had more pleasure in sex, and I mean in every way, than when we decided to stop . . . taking precautions . . . and tried to have a child. You. It surprised the hell out of us.

PETER That's nice. I'm glad you told me that.

CHARLEY And we keep getting surprised . . . You must know, Peter, that life is not a continuing peak experience . . . It's often giving up intense heat for continuing warmth . . . It's sex often as an act of compassion and comfort and not just adoring desire . . . It's on occasion to have a few martinis and come home, even though it's the last thing in the world you want to do . . . (*He looks at his son's small and slightly sad smile*) I don't persuade you.

PETER Do you persuade yourself?

CHARLEY (*A long pause . . . Shakes his head*) Not entirely.

PETER Thanks . . . The other night Melinda and I were at a party at her parents'. One hour into the party and half the guests were pushing the other half into the pool with their clothes on . . . all loaded. And God knows which wife belonged to which husband. Melinda and I held each other very close when we got home and she said, "Dear God, let's never let that happen to us."

CHARLEY (*Smiling*) Your generation presumably advocates anarchy. At the pool there, that was their small fling at anarchy, which enables them to go back to work Monday morning . . . You know, Peter, the best most of us can manage is to preserve some little anarchy within the shape and form of our lives.

PETER (*After a moment*) Where's the little anarchy in your life, Dad?

CHARLEY (*Looks at him a long time, knowing he is near the truth . . . then passes it off*) Haven't you noticed that occasionally I wear loud bow ties? And when things get really rough, I go to some far away beach and walk naked.

PETER   And the joy? Where's that? Pure sensual joy? (CHARLEY *just looks at him . . . His son is needling him where it hurts*) Wearing bow ties and walking naked on a beach are not going to be enough for me. (*Moving on, more daring, and more loving*) May I say something else?

CHARLEY   Sure.

PETER   I think you're too reconciled in your life and in your work. I wrote a paper on you once in college, on your short stories. Do you realize that every single one of your couples gets back together again in the end? Half of them don't belong together. But you bring them crawling back as though you had invented marriage and had to justify it under all circumstances . . . You and Mother would would have been much better off divorced years ago.

CHARLEY   Now, Peter . . .

PETER   (*Running right over*)   But you stayed together, I suppose for us children.

CHARLEY   Come on, Peter, stop it. It's simply not—

PETER   (*Pressing on*)   —What's real in those stories, Dad, is the ache and longing and pain. Sometimes I don't know how Mother could read your stories, the pain is so real and obviously personal.

CHARLEY   (*Trying to be patient*)   Peter, my sister and I also thought our parents should have been divorced. No children think their parents love each other as children understand love.

PETER   Dad, how many of your friends are faithful to the wives they presumably love? God, I can't imagine being unfaithful to Melinda. It would make me sick to even think of it.

CHARLEY   I'm glad. I'm very glad. But you mustn't be so contemptuous of the way other people manage their lives. Life is just not that simple, Peter. It is for you now, and I'm glad, and I envy you, and I wouldn't have it any other way. But you must understand we all felt much the same way when we were your age.

PETER   You couldn't have!

CHARLEY   (*Flaring a moment*)   You know I get very tired of being told what I felt or didn't feel at your age! . . . I'm sorry, but my college notebooks were full of wonderful quotations. Hemingway: "A woman should be adored or abandoned." . . . Someone else: "Let it be high noon, and then let it be midnight." I spent a night in jail for rioting in college, protesting the firing of a liberal professor . . . It enrages you to think that we could have been the same. Because if we were, and ended up as we have, there's more than a chance you'll end up the same way. (PETER *is cowed by his father's "sounding off"* . . . *Almost has to look at the sight indirectly* . . . *not straight on*) Therefore you must desperately insist that you are different. Therefore you will end up different . . . Look, I hope to Christ you do. But you do not have a patent on the search for meaningfulness in life or love, and the frustrations resulting therefrom. The middle-aged man is much more fed up with things than you are. And he's in a much worse spot, because he can't feed himself simple solutions, because he knows they won't work. He's got the same anguish, but no clear answers, and time is running the hell out on him. And while he's desperately trying to salvage something before it's too late, the kids sneer at him and say, "You sold out. You blew it." And then he says to them, because he's hurt, "Wait till it's your turn!" And then . . . (*He stops himself. He realizes he has given away more of his true feelings than he meant to*) I'm sorry.

PETER (*Different meaning*) I'm sorry too, Dad.

CHARLEY I hope you make it . . . I'll do whatever I can to help . . . But don't get the idea I'm not trying to make it too . . . Show me your film.

PETER Joy, Dad . . . That's all . . . Think about it.
(CHARLEY *looks at him a long time and nods his head . . . The film begins . . . For a few moments they watch it together . . . Then* PETER *leaves . . .*

The title: "I'm home!" Then . . . "A Film by Peter Potter."

The film is a lyrical evocation of a young man's coming home in the evening to the girl he loves. We start with his getting off a bus, weaving and skipping his way through the crowd of other people coming home from work.

He stops and buys an evening newspaper. He jogs to his next destination, a fruit and flower stand, where he buys a loosely wrapped small bunch of flowers . . . very cheap. And he continues on his way, breaking into a trot as he turns into his own street . . . a street in the Village . . . Spring . . . a

*a few trees out . . . flowers on the window ledges,
people sitting on the stoops.*

*On the run, he turns into his own quaint building,
looks for mail, sees none, goes in. He bounds up the
stairs, opens his door, enters his apartment, which is
only one large room with just the essentials . . . He
calls out for Melinda (silent film). "I'm home." Sees
a simple table, simply set. Looks in the tiny kitchen,
but she isn't there. He shucks off his coat and proceeds to the bathroom, where the water is running.
He goes in.*

*It is a large old-fashioned bathroom. Melinda is
taking a steamy bath. She drapes a wet washcloth
across her breasts in pretended modesty. He presents her elaborately with the flowers. She laughs
and reaches out for them (playacting). He kneels
down beside the tub and kisses her. The wash cloth
slips into the water. He continues to kiss her while
she's holding the flowers, giggling, not having any
place to put them . . . He starts to stroke her
wet breast, still kissing her and enjoying her awkward protests . . . His hand goes under the water,
shirt-sleeve and all, and she laughs as his mouth goes
to her neck . . . As she laughs delightedly, she lets
go of her flowers and they scatter on the water . . .
We draw back quickly and stop action on the scene,
the girl in the tub, the young man kissing and fon-
dling her . . . and the flowers floating on the sur-
face. . .*

*End of film . . . Obviously the film has had a
deep effect on* CHARLEY *. . . He looks over at*
BARBARA *at her table . . . She looks at him . . .
They hold the look for a very long moment . . .
Then . . .)*

CHARLEY (*Indicating the view offstage*) Marvelous spot, isn't it?

BARBARA Yes, beautiful.

CHARLEY All that ocean. (*He gets up . . . moves his chair towards the open space in the center . . .*) Reminds me of the beach at Ipswich.

BARBARA (*A small smile*) All beaches remind you of the beach at Ipswich. (*She gets up, and during following moves her chair towards center . . . also a small stool which has been at her table*) But this Godforsaken shack. "Fully equipped."

CHARLEY (*Determined not to be put off by anything*) Well, it's fully equipped with the sun and the sea and the beach, this deck and a double bed. What else do we need?

BARBARA (*Arranging her chair and stool before she sits in sun to rest*) Have you sat on that double bed?
(BARBARA *is on edge, but succeeds in being bantering*)

CHARLEY Well, we'll drag the mattress out here on the deck and sleep under the stars. We've done that before. (*He makes a big gesture*)

BARBARA When we go into the village, remind me to get some ammonia. I want to scrub this place down. And some ant powder. How much are we paying for this place?
(*In a sense she is trying to de-fuse the situation with down-to-earth concerns*)

CHARLEY (*Lounging in his chair next to hers*) I don't

remember. I don't care. We didn't come down here to keep house.

BARBARA That's fine for you to say. But I can't prepare meals in that grime.

CHARLEY We'll get a charcoal broiler, and I'll cook out here. The simple life.

BARBARA If we're going to sleep out here and cook out here, there's no reason for us to have paid a fortune for this shack.

CHARLEY We're paying a fortune for the chance to be alone for the first time in God knows when. I put my watch in my suitcase. And I'm not going to look at it again for a week. If we're hungry, we'll eat. Whenever. If we're sleepy, we'll sleep. Whenever. If we want to make love, we'll make love. Whenever.
  (*He nuzzles her neck playfully*)

BARBARA Well, I'm sleepy. So I'll sleep.
CHARLEY Let's take our clothes off and go swimming skinny.

BARBARA Oh, now, Charley. Come on. There are people.

CHARLEY There are no people. I asked the man for a place on a deserted beach where I could make love to my wife for a week.

BARBARA And he's probably lying up there in the long grass right now with binoculars . . . A few minutes ago there was a boat out there . . . and there are planes.

CHARLEY (*Looks up*) What the hell can they see?

BARBARA They can see.

CHARLEY You overrate the size of my cock, dear girl, if you think they can see it from up there.

BARBARA Shhhhh. They can see.

CHARLEY You think they can hear too?
(*He holds her hand for a moment, then moves it towards his crotch*)

BARBARA (*Drawing her hand away*) Come on now, stop it. You're some kind of maniac. No sooner do we get inside that door this morning than you start pawing me and wanting to practically rape me on that filthy floor . . . And now you want me to sit around and admire your amazing virility.

CHARLEY It's not amazing. I just want to show you what you do to me. You and the beach . . . (*She looks at him . . . "Tell me another." He leans close to her*) Do you remember the first time at Ipswich?

BARBARA Come on now, Charley. I want to rest. I've had a hell of a rough time trying to get ready for the anniversary party. It was crazy coming down here just before it, but since we are here, let me get some rest . . . first. I'll make a date with you for later.

CHARLEY (*Playfully*) Remember what the doctor said to you before we were married. It's a fleeting impulse. I.O.U.'s are not much good.

BARBARA You know, Charley, you've become a damned chatterer.

CHARLEY Become? I've always been. Just keeping contact. Nature abhors a vacuum . . . Remember when we went to Europe on our honeymoon and we saw all those middle-aged couples sitting at tables and staring into space and saying nothing . . . And you reached over to me and said, "Promise me, Charley, you'll always keep talking. Anything. Something. Just keep talking to me."

BARBARA (*Smiling*) Yes. I remember.

CHARLEY But that's all right. You just rest a while, and I'll sit here doing nothing.
(*After a moment, he put his hand on her . . . just to keep contact*)

BARBARA That's not doing nothing.

CHARLEY Just keeping contact. (*He is quiet for a moment . . . then*) You know we've never been together on a piano bench. George says that's very exciting.

BARBARA I'm sure George has had more girls in more bizarre places than the piano bench.

CHARLEY You're not above some bizarre places yourself . . . George said the only advice he gave his son when he got married was to save doing it from the chandeliers until they are forty . . . For weeks after he told me that, I looked at every chandelier and tried to figure out how you'd manage it . . . Have you an idea how you'd do it?

BARBARA It doesn't interest me enough to try to figure it out—and with your arthritis I suggest you forget about it.

CHARLEY Women, by and large, have very little curiosity about those things, don't they? . . . Men have much more fun with their feelings of sex than women do.

BARBARA Oh, I don't know.

CHARLEY Like I remember at my fraternity house in college, there was a guy who always got the most incredible erection after a good meal. It became the pride of the fraternity. We used to invite people to dinner just to show him off. (BARBARA *smiles and shakes her head*) Just from eating a big dinner. Bill . . . Bill. What the hell was his last name? I wonder if it still happens to him.

BARBARA What are you going to do, write him and ask him?

CHARLEY Maloney, Bill Maloney. Actually quite a small guy otherwise.

BARBARA You sound like a bunch of kids with a toy. Look at my Yo-Yo.

CHARLEY Did I ever tell you I had my first orgasm while I was taking a math exam at prep school. There I was trying to figure out the square root of some damned number, and bam!

BARBARA You told me. On our first date.

CHARLEY (*He kisses her hand, and keeps holding it*) When we first met, when I'd have to go to New York to see my folks and then come back to you in Boston, I used to start getting excited around New London, and stay that way till after we'd been together in your apartment three hours later.

BARBARA You used to say it was Stanford and four hours.

CHARLEY Well, I'm getting older and three hours seems like a more reasonable time . . . You'd be there waiting, and all bathed, and if it was winter, a fire going . . . wearing that wonderful red flannel robe and nothing else. Whatever happened to that robe?

BARBARA The moths got it.

CHARLEY Thanks.

BARBARA Well, you asked.

CHARLEY It was a rhetorical question. When François Villon asked, "Where are the snows of yesteryear?" he didn't want some smartass to say, "They melted." (*Close to her* . . .) Let's make love now. Then take a nap. Then go swimming skinny and make love in the water. You taught me that . . . Then come back and eat . . . and . . . see what happens.

BARBARA (*Less kidding—but saying it—but without annoyance*) Not now, Charley.

CHARLEY Men are much more easily put off than women. Kinsey says that a woman can talk to her three best friends on the phone without breaking stride.

BARBARA Your mind is full of the damnedest most useless sexual information.

CHARLEY You used to love to have me chatter away about sex. Shock you . . . amuse you. You used to laugh so much. It used to excite you, me going on with nonsense like this.

BARBARA It amused me.

74

CHARLEY It excited you. I proved it to you once with unmistakable evidence. Just by talking to you. No hands.

BARBARA Well, thank God I don't remember.

CHARLEY It was a motel outside of Marblehead, July 18, Sunday, 3:33 in the afternoon. And what I was saying was—
 (*He leans towards her*)

BARBARA —I don't want to hear it. I'm a middle-aged matron now. Old enough to be the mother of the girl you were talking to.

CHARLEY (*That she should think this is infinitely sad to him*) You don't look any different to me . . . Someone once said, "Men are only boys grown tall." I look at so many women, and I can't see any "girl" left in them . . . where they were ever girls. I have no trouble seeing it in you. (*She is touched by this, but still defensive*) That's one of the great things about you.

BARBARA Name another.

CHARLEY Well . . .
 (*He pauses a moment*)

BARBARA Time's up.

CHARLEY (*Can she really feel so unappreciated?*) Come on. Lots of things . . . A lot of things. (*A small touch of reassurance . . . He almost absent-mindedly strokes her wrist . . . then kidding . . .*) That used to drive you crazy.

BARBARA It still does when I'm trying to sleep.

CHARLEY (*Stops stroking . . . but leaves his hand on hers*) The new thing, I understand, is vibrators. (*She shudders at the idea*) Feathers, they say, can be exciting . . . (*He reaches up and casually rubs his finger over the lobe of her ear*) That was never one of your spots . . . I'm sensitive on the back of my knees . . . some days . . . Some days I'm not. (*He touches the back of his knees*) Today I am, if you'd care to try. (*She doesn't care to try*) The kids say pot makes it something extra . . . I'm willing to try anything. Maybe when I'm fifty. Chandeliers at forty-five. Pot at fifty. Vibrators at fifty-five. Group gropes at fifty-eight. Though I can't imagine anyone wanting to grope me at fifty-eight. I speak for myself. You will remain eternally gropable. (*He looks at her a long time. The Game is over . . . finally he speaks*) Barbara? (*There is no answer*) What's the matter? (*She just looks at him*) What?

BARBARA I don't know.

CHARLEY (*Gently, wondering*) We haven't been together in weeks.

BARBARA I know. (*Evasive*) All the preparations for the anniversary . . . I've been . . . tired.

CHARLEY That's why I thought if we got away.

BARBARA I'm sorry. (*She looks at him a long moment, a sad frown on her face*) I've been terrified of this trip, Charley.

CHARLEY Why?
(*He moves comfortingly towards her*)

BARBARA (*Shies away a little*) I don't know. The whole thing. It's such a set-up. (*She looks at him, hoping for help*) Your sentimental and nostalgic presents every fifteen minutes on the plane. Then this shack, miles away from anyplace.

CHARLEY I'm sorry it's so . . .
(*He gestures "ratty"*)

BARBARA There's something so desperate about it. (*She looks at him, questioning. He won't admit it*) As though we were taking some kind of exam, and I know I'm going to flunk it. (*He makes another comforting gesture towards her*) We're down here, aren't we, trying to see if there's any reason for renewing our vows?

CHARLEY (*Uncomfortable*) Oh, come on now, Barbara. We're just having a vacation, at last.

BARBARA Charley, let's be honest. We're not going to come out of this alive, so let's be honest.

CHARLEY (*Making a warm, reassuring move towards her. His response is always to touch, to give physical comfort . . .*) Barbara . . .
(*He stops*)

BARBARA I just feel it's so desperate and so sad . . . Not just this. But the way it's been for so long. I tried to say it last time we made love. I asked you if you could only make love to me when you were a little high. I was a coward. I waited till you were asleep, and then I only whispered it.

CHARLEY I wasn't asleep.

BARBARA You didn't answer.

CHARLEY I . . .

BARBARA (*Cutting him off*) I don't want an answer . . . It's just that lately I get the feeling that we're not

77

just making love. We're trying to prove something. "I do love my wife, and I'm going to prove it by making love to her. See how much and how well I'm making love to her."

CHARLEY Barbara . . .

BARBARA (*Running on*) Only you have to have a couple of drinks to make a quick connection, to by-pass all we really are till our bodies take over.

CHARLEY Barbara, that's not so.

BARBARA (*Hardly listening or hearing . . . she has been wound up for a long time, and she's going . . . but just spilling . . . not vindictive . . . almost fearful that if she stops, she'll be horrified at what she's been saying . . .*) We used to go through all we really are and end up making love. Now it's nostalgia and martinis . . . Oh, I'm saying terrible things I never thought I'd say, and I'm jumbling them all together . . . But we are here . . . (*Suddenly loud . . . blurting it out*) And I must say these things! (CHARLEY *realizes that it is not the time to question or challenge . . . This may be irrational, what she's saying, but it's the truth of how she feels . . . he moves again to hold her, she shies away*) . . . I have the feeling that we're two systems of nerve ends, which we manipulate expertly, desperately. Your hands and mouth are everywhere, expertly playing the instrument. But where are you? Where's Charley? And where am I? . . . You move on, desperately trying to reestablish some intimacy. But not with me, Barbara . . . One night, so long ago, I said while we were making love, "Oh, I love you so." You should have seen your eyes. Your body and your arms responded tenderly, but your eyes opened in shock and fright at that kind of intimacy . . . I can't tell you how indecent I feel sometimes in bed with you. We've glided by each other for days or weeks, never touching. I don't mean physically. And then suddenly there we are in bed, naked, servicing each other . . . And I sometimes feel like a whore with a stranger . . . A stranger who then suddenly tries to prove he's in love with me . . . But I can't respond, except physically, because I don't know anything about him . . . Oh, I'm sorry.

(*She puts both her hands over her mouth, shocked that she has said all this*)

CHARLEY Barbara, you make me sound completely insensitive.

BARBARA Oh, no, love, you're not that. And I didn't mean that. I'm saying it all wrong. No wonder you never want to talk . . . What do I mean? . . . I know you don't always have to be high, because sometimes we make love in the morning . . . but why do I have these feelings?

CHARLEY (*Gently*) Each time . . . most times when I make love to you, I feel closer to you . . . more intimate, more deeply connected, after. It is a way of reestablishing intimacy, contact. It is not the only way. But it *is* a way.

BARBARA I guess I sense you would feel this way with any woman.

CHARLEY I might. (*She looks at him*) But the point is that it is with *you, Barbara, my wife*, I am feeling it. And so I feel closer to *you* . . . and to myself for a while.

BARBARA So often I feel more lonely after . . . Once in a restaurant, I saw you at one of those tables in the

79

corner with a lovely woman, perhaps one of your writers. And you were talking, talking. I couldn't hear you, but I could see. The way we used to talk. Your eyes were looking at her, into her, not just towards her. And I said something to myself, and it shocked me. I said, "I wish he'd go to bed with her and talk to me." (*Saddened by this,* CHARLEY *moves again to hold her*) No, please. I want to talk.

CHARLEY (*Harsh*)   I want to hold you, for God's sake! Let me touch you. I just want to hold you!
>   (*The tone shocks her. Is this what he has been talking about? His instinctive need for physical intimacy and communication through bodies . . . They sit together, huddled, his arm around her . . .*)

BARBARA (*After a long moment*)   I hate marriage. I hate what it has done to me. I'm not me. I'm a nice person, loving, warm, generous, understanding . . . when I'm not married. We used to share our loneliness, our miseries. Love each other for the sharing. But now we cause each other some of the loneliness and misery. How can we tell each other that? . . . When you were going through that thing with Maria, and I knew it, the unmarried part of me said, "He's torn and miserable. Why doesn't he come and tell me, and I'd comfort him the way I used to, and he'd love me for the talking?" . . . The married part of me hated you and her . . . Who do you talk to these days, Charley? (*He smiles*) You hate marriage too, Charley.

CHARLEY   No.

BARBARA   You like the idea of marriage. But you hate what it turns out to be . . . I've wanted to shout at you, "For Christ's sake, be a good sport! This happens to everyone. Settle! Don't always be considering the alternatives!" . . . I envy you your longing to be in love, intensely, adoringly. I don't seem to feel that need, and I can't respond to it. It makes me feel ridiculous. Grotesque . . . A couple of times I wished I were dying because I thought it might give you that intensity of feeling you want. I fantasied it for months once. And I wondered why you weren't nicer to me when you knew I was dying. (*She smiles at the ridiculousness of the concept*) You've wished me dead sometimes, haven't you, Charley?

CHARLEY   Come on.

BARBARA   I've wished you dead. It seemed the only way we could ever get out of this . . . Lovers are lousy husbands. That's not fair. You're a good husband in many ways. But that unhappy, disappointed lover keeps messing up the works.

CHARLEY   You seem so . . . I don't know, so intent on killing his passion.

BARBARA   Oh, God, I know. You've thought me a cold bitch.

CHARLEY   No. But I've wondered so often when you turn away . . . I've wondered about . . . about your insensitivity. (*Quickly*) Not to my feelings or needs, but to both our feelings and needs. As though something within you had said, "No, I'm a grown woman. That's all over." . . . One of the great things about us, when we were starting out, was our accessibility, our availability to each other . . . in every way . . . *I* don't always feel like making love. But I do feel the need to be closer to you, somehow, some way. We've been so distant I begin to feel I'll freeze to death without some contact. And I know that in a few moments, I *will* feel like . . . You don't seem to want to give the moment a chance. When you reach for me, I find it tremendously exciting, immediately exciting. But when I move towards you, so often it . . . (*He stops. He has said all this most gently, tentatively*)

BARBARA   I don't know. I guess I'm unconsciously trying to flag you down. To shout, "Hey, Charley, it's me. Barbara. Age forty-two. Not your girl. You scared me because I knew I couldn't be your girl . . . your bride. All brides die, Charley . . . I felt it was fantasy time. Charades. (*They sit quietly for a moment . . .*) I've thought about divorce a lot, Charley. Seriously. Why the hell should two people stay together for twenty-three years? . . . Why should two people go along like two Goddamned railroad tracks side by side into Eternity . . . I don't think we're the least bit compatible any more . . . practically nothing in common . . . Your mother suggested we take up double solitaire. I almost laughed in her face, because what else have we been playing these last years? . . . Charley, if you're staying with me because you're afraid it will break me up if you leave . . . Don't . . . You've seemed so unhappy sometimes that I've wished you would get up the courage to call it quits. Just when I've thought you might, you start making that desperate love to me . . . I won't fleece you, because I have money of my own, and Sylvia says she'll take me into her shop . . . and . . . and I can take care of myself. I may be a little lonely, but not as lonely as I've been these last Goddamned years. (*She breaks down and starts to cry . . . sobbing.* CHARLEY *holds her tighter . . . pained . . . comforting . . . he kisses her hair*) Don't! . . . Go away! (*He just holds her comforting. His eyes closed at the pain . . . hers and his. At the moment he feels infinitely tender towards her . . . as she subsides, he moves closer to her, touching her face, caressing . . . a mixture of compassion and passion. Draws into herself)* No. *(She frowns)* Why?

CHARLEY *(Calmly)* Because I want to.

BARBARA Why?

CHARLEY I don't know.

BARBARA What'll it prove?

CHARLEY Nothing.

BARBARA I want to talk.

CHARLEY We've talked.

BARBARA I've talked . . . Are you afraid that if you talked it would be too awful? *(He smiles sadly at the idea, and continues to touch her)* Dear Charley . . . two years from now, if we stay together that long . . . and at this moment . . . I'm not sure I care if we do . . . you'll drag me down here to try to recapture whatever it is we've got at this moment.

CHARLEY Maybe.

BARBARA I'm telling you now, I won't come. (CHARLEY *starts to unbutton her blouse . . . She looks at him, smiling sadly . . . She touches his head . . .)* You won't find anything there you haven't found a thousand times before.

> *(He smiles, as he continues . . . The lights slowly fade on them . . .)*

The End

ROBERT ANDERSON was born in New York City in 1917, attended Phillips Exeter Academy and was graduated from Harvard University in 1939. During the following three years, earning his M.A. at Harvard and completing courses toward a Ph.D., he wrote twenty-one one-act plays, wrote the book, music and lyrics for college musicals, did drama criticism, and taught drama and writing courses. He then served for four years as a naval officer in the Pacific during World War II; during that time he wrote *Come Marching Home*, which won the National Theater Conference prize for the best play written by a serviceman on overseas duty.

In 1953 Mr. Anderson's first Broadway play, *Tea and Sympathy*, opened, and became the longest-running hit in the twenty-one-year history of The Playwrights' Company. On the night before *Tea and Sympathy* opened in New Haven, Mr. Anderson became a member of The Playwrights' Company, which also produced his *All Summer Long* in 1954 and *Silent Night, Lonely Night* in 1959. Prior to the production of *Tea and Sympathy*, he wrote extensively for television and radio, and started the playwriting courses at the Actors Studio and the American Wing Theatre, where he taught for four years. He was one of the original members of The New Dramatists, and was president of the group for one year. In 1967, Mr. Anderson's new comedy, *You Know I Can't Hear You When the Water's Running*, opened on Broadway, and was followed a year later by *I Never Sang for My Father*, which also enjoyed a lengthy run. Mr. Anderson has written many original screenplays, notably *The Nun's Story* and *The Sand Pebbles*, and has successfully adapted two of his plays to the screen, *Tea and Sympathy* and *I Never Sang for My Father*. The latter won the Writer's Guild award for Best Screenplay (Drama) and received an Academy Award nomination for best screenplay in 1970.

Recently, Mr. Anderson was a member of the faculty of The Salzburgh Seminar in American Studies, and is currently the President of The Dramatists Guild. He is married to actress Teresa Wright and they live in Bridgewater, Conn.